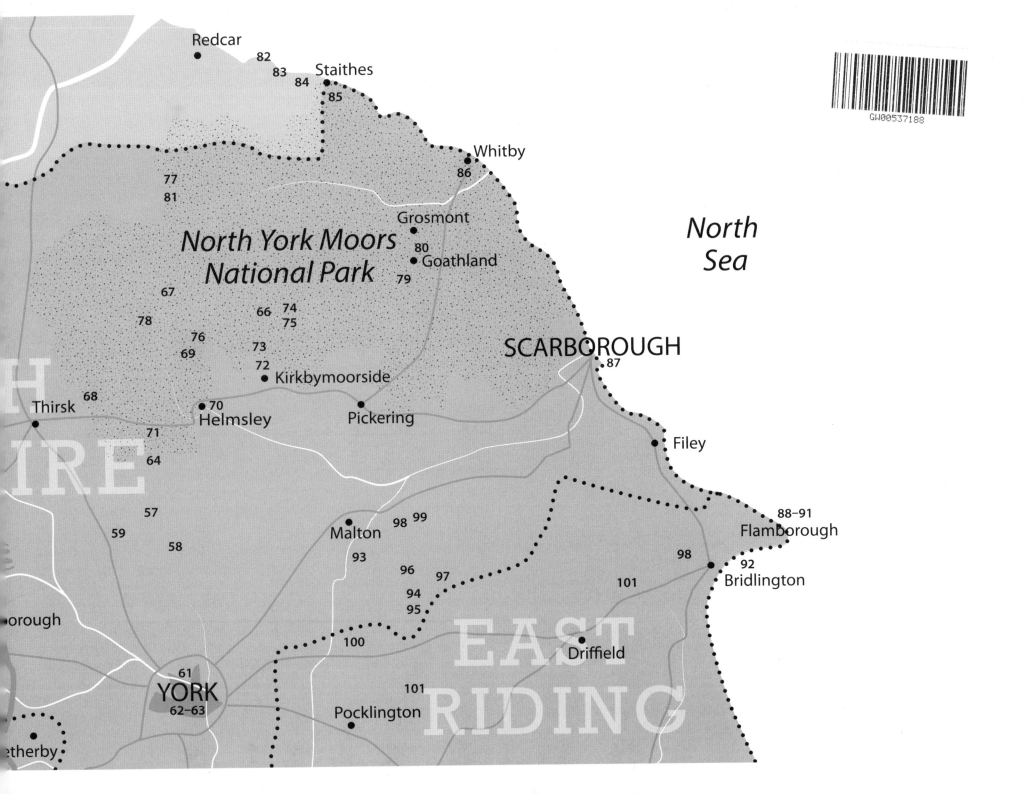

Redcar

82
83
Staithes
84
85

Whitby
86

North
Sea

77
81

Grosmont
80
Goathland
79

North York Moors
National Park

67

66  74
75

78

76
69

73

72
Kirkbymoorside

SCARBOROUGH
87

Thirsk
68
70
Helmsley

Pickering

Filey

71

64

57

Malton
98  99

59

93

58

96
97

94
95

88–91
Flamborough

98

92
Bridlington

101

100

Driffield

61
YORK
62–63

101

Pocklington

EAST
RIDING

etherby

# YORKSHIRE LANDSCAPES

## A Photographic Tour of England's Largest County

Doug Kennedy

WINDgather PRESS

Windgather Press is an imprint of Oxbow Books

Published in the United Kingdom in 2017 by
OXBOW BOOKS
The Old Music Hall, 106–108 Cowley Road, Oxford OX4 1JE

and in the United States by
OXBOW BOOKS
1950 Lawrence Road, Havertown, PA 19083

© Doug Kennedy 2017

Hardback Edition: ISBN 978-1-909686-97-7
Digital Edition: ISBN 978-1-909686-98-4

A CIP record for this book is available from the British Library

Typeset in the UK by Frabjous Books
Printed in India by Replika Press Pvt. Ltd.

For a complete list of Windgather titles, please contact:

United Kingdom
Oxbow Books
Telephone (01865) 241249
Fax (01865) 794449
Email: oxbow@oxbowbooks.com
www.oxbowbooks.com

United States of America
Oxbow Books
Telephone (800) 791-9354
Fax (610) 853-9146
Email: queries@casemateacademic.com
www.casemateacademic.com/oxbow

Oxbow Books is part of the Casemate Group

All photographs have been taken by Doug Kennedy (www.doug-kennedy.com)

# Contents

# Foreword

Yorkshire is a region in the north of England with its own particular cultural identity. For a long time, it was by far the largest county in England, stretching some 100 miles from Carnforth, only a few miles from the Irish Sea in the west, to the North Sea coast in the east; and from the River Tees in the North to the City of Sheffield in the south. With a resident population of about six million, it has been administratively expedient to divide Yorkshire into Ridings, and later into smaller counties, but when asked, people will still say that they come from Yorkshire. In addition, the twenty million annual visitors to its two large National Parks and its countless landscape and heritage attractions certainly know where they are.

Doug Kennedy has taken on a considerable challenge in attempting to portray the enormous extent and variety of landscapes across Yorkshire, from the remote limestone Dales to the industrial flatlands of Humberside, to the gentle Wolds and the Plain of York. I believe that he has succeeded, capturing the splendour of all four corners of the county and much of the best that lies between. His stunning images are arranged in a way that imparts the delight of discovery with every turn of the page. Having lived in Scarborough for almost fifty years, I find Doug's book a wonderful window through which I can appreciate and enjoy places that I know and love, along with others that I hardly know at all. I believe that *Yorkshire Landscapes* will be loved by natives and visitors alike, and bring joy to many who now live at a distance.

Cecil B. Snell

# Introduction

Yorkshire covers a large proportion of Northern England and, in my view, contains the greatest variety of landscapes of any region in Great Britain and some of the loveliest. I have tried to include images of all the main landscape types and was so spoiled for choice that it has been very difficult to hone the collection down to 112 pages. So this pictorial exploration covers the entire Yorkshire region, extending into Redcar and Cleveland which were part of Yorkshire until the administrative county changes in 1972. The accompanying text not only explains the pictures, but describes how the landscape evolved along with some history and anecdotes.

Our journey starts in South Yorkshire where the open heather-clad Pennine moors contrast sharply with the industrial heartlands of Sheffield and Doncaster. Here we explore the industrial heritage as well as the open landscapes and, now that the smokestacks of its heavy industrial past have gone, encounter some unexpected beauty.

In West Yorkshire, the huge conurbations around Leeds, Bradford and Huddersfield blanket much of the lowlands, but the land rises up the many river valleys where mills, houses and heather mingle in surprising ways, opening onto vast open moors where you can get away from it all. Here we encounter the Brontës, the location of *Last of the Summer Wine* and places like Hebden Bridge, where a smoky industrial heritage has been gradually transformed, as communities seek social and environmental sustainability.

Industry has had far less impact on the open limestone landscapes of the Yorkshire Dales, where pale grey rock and green grass dominate the high rounded hills that rise from steep-sided valleys. Here, sparkling becks tumble through picturesque villages and we find limestone pavements, disappearing rivers, the best caving in Britain and England's highest pub with its amazing views.

Between the Dales and the Moors lies the green and pleasant Plain of York, which from Roman times until the Civil War saw many major battles fought around its castles and the walled City of York itself. We visit York Minster and browse among settlements, waterways and backwaters, seeking out the character and lie of the land.

The North Yorkshire Moors straddle the north-east, offering more heather-covered upland, but also valleys and settlements of enormous character. The moors stretch to the spectacular North Sea coast where the Cleveland Way traverses 500 foot cliff tops, then drops to sea level, where fishing boats are moored in picturesque harbours.

Heading south, we explore the gentle landscape of the Yorkshire Wolds, beloved of David Hockney, before completing our tour in the flat lands of Holderness and along the mighty River Humber.

This book attempts to capture the essential character of Yorkshire landscapes through the 140-odd images that have been selected not only for their subject, but also for how they fit together visually to paint a colourful picture that is true to reality. If it brings back memories or whets the reader's appetite to visit Yorkshire, it will have succeeded in its aim.

## South Yorkshire

This is the smallest of Yorkshire's administrative counties, stretching from the Lincolnshire fens in the east to the Pennine moors and the Derbyshire Peak District in the west. For two centuries, South Yorkshire was at the centre of England's coal and steel industries, with dozens of collieries blackening the countryside around Barnsley, Rotherham and Doncaster. Hatfield Colliery near Rotherham was the last to close in 2015, a demise that was unimaginable prior to the miners' strike in 1985. Similarly, the huge steel industry in Sheffield and Rotherham that used to roar and glow like Dante's Inferno in Brightside, and which turned the drizzle so acid that it made holes in ladies' stockings, has reduced substantially and become a lot cleaner. As the heavy industries closed, so did all the hundreds of smaller businesses that serviced them or used the steel to manufacture cutlery, canisters and car parts. One result is that the county's air is now clear, its rain not acid and its once highly polluted rivers that ran red with industrial waste are largely clean. In addition, the pit heads and slag heaps of the coal mines are being converted into green spaces, and once-polluted industrial ponds now teem with wildlife.

However, in South Yorkshire the contrast between the low-lying east and the upland west, between the industrial urban valleys and the wild moors, remains dramatic. Coming from the east, the land ascends gradually through gritty industrial towns and villages, many of which run into each other as they ascend the river valleys. The classic millstone grit building material, once mostly black from the soot in the air creating the atmosphere of 'dark satanic mills', has now been cleaned and restored to its natural stone colour in many places. The area remains industrial at its core, although lighter industrial and service-based businesses have replaced many of the mills and foundries and steel-capped boots and miners' helmets have been replaced by high visibility jackets and hard hats.

Sheffield is known as a city on seven hills, and as you head west from the city centre, the land rises to well over 1,000 feet, becoming open moorland which merges into the Peak District National Park. There is still industry to be found in the valleys of Stocksbridge and Penistone, but the views over rounded heather-covered moors are mostly uninterrupted by smoke and chimneys.

**Opposite:** Heather-clad Pennine moors in the west of the county with the Holme Moss radio transmitter and lorries crossing the Woodhead Pass in the distance.
**Above:** This flowery field sits atop the north side of the Don Valley near Cadeby, with views over Conisbrough towards Rotherham.

# The River Don

South Yorkshire's main river is the Don, whose source lies in the moors above Penistone in the north-west. It is joined by the Dearne, flowing from Barnsley in the north, and the Rother that serves Rotherham in the south. These rivers link most of the county's industrial towns, including Sheffield, Rotherham, Barnsley and Doncaster, and serve the many factories before exiting the county as a pair of ramrod-straight canals that empty into the rivers Ouse and Trent. It was the combination of good coal and plentiful water that enabled industries to grow in South Yorkshire, so the river valleys are highly urbanised, often leaving no space between settlements. From the Industrial Revolution through to the late 20th century, the clear and clean water of the Don as it left the high moors became discoloured and poisoned before it had passed through Sheffield, and it still had a long journey to endure through the industrial heartlands. The old saying, 'Where there's muck there's brass!', was writ large and the industries that caused the pollution brought jobs, wealth and pride to the region, which has had to adapt painfully to a changing world. Now, environmental controls and the loss of heavy industry have allowed the rivers to run clear again and settlement ponds have turned into wildlife reserves where fish, birds and otters thrive.

Since the Industrial Revolution, South Yorkshire's rivers have been manipulated, redirected and dammed to provide drinking water and the needs of industry. Dams across valleys on the Pennine slopes block valleys to store water, and the river's passage through the towns is interrupted by many weirs, built to supply mills, foundries and power the cutlers' grinding wheels. Rivers were channelled with stone and concrete and, as early as the 17th century, the Don was entirely diverted east of Doncaster to flow through a canal on a new course to join the River Ouse, instead of the Trent.

**Left:** Conisbrough Castle: This Norman castle with its tall keep was abandoned as a stronghold in the 15th century owing to some the land it sits upon subsiding, but is still in quite good condition despite surrounding industry and housing.

**Above:** Green fields cloak the slopes of the Don valley; here looking north towards Swinton and Barnsley.

**Page 8:** One of Sheffield's hills is Parkwood Springs, rising steeply a few hundred yards from the city centre. The upper section is now a park containing nature reserves and with views across Sheffield in all directions. This image is over the north of the city and the Don Valley towards the Pennine Hills.

**Page 9:** The River Don at Attercliffe in Sheffield with the Cathedral in the distance. The river's transformation is remarkable, thanks in part to projects like The Living Don which are working to restore and enhance its health and wildlife. (See http://www.wildsheffield.com/)

# Sheffield's Countryside

Sheffield is one of England's great industrial cities, but heading west from the town centre past the university, the industrial scene is left behind to be replaced by a dramatic landscape of green fields, deep valleys and, in the late summer, a carpet of purple heather. One route from the city is the A57 which passes through the Rivelin Valley (right) whose steep sides are a rugged mix of forest and heather, presaging the open expanses of Hallam and Bradfield Moors. Dry-stone walls constructed of blocks of millstone grit define every field and steep lanes link the valleys, most of which contain reservoirs. There are few settlements of any size in the higher places and the rambler can walk for many miles and enjoy uninterrupted views of heath-covered moor and the sky.

**Below Left:** St Nicholas Church in High Bradfield seen across one of the local tiled roofs.
**Below Right:** An old way stone at a crossroads on White Lee Moor.
**Right:** Stanage Pole, which marks the border between Derbyshire and South Yorkshire above the Redmires Reservoirs.
**Opposite:** The Rivelin Valley, west of Sheffield from the pub at Lodge Moor.

**Page 12:** The view from Hallam Moor over the Redmires Reservoirs to Sheffield and beyond.
**Page 13:** The expanse of Hallam Moor with Stanage Lodge in lonely isolation.

BRADFIELD

SHEFFIELD

R M

WIGHTWIZZLE

BOLSTERSTONE

## Stanage Edge

Located in the Peak District National Park where it forms the county border for much of its length, Stanage Edge is our largest gritstone cliff at approximately 4 miles in length and 458m (1,500 feet) at its highest point. The area is popular for walking, but is particularly valued for climbing with hundreds of rock climbing routes designed for all levels of ability. From the top, there are extensive views across the Derbyshire Peaks, over Hathersage, Bamford and up the Hope Valley to Castleton and the bleak heights of Kinder Scout. The image on the left looks northwards along the Edge, with walkers descending the steep path to Hathersage in the foreground.

Access to Stanage Edge was not always open as it falls within the North Lees Estate where it was part of a private grouse moor patrolled by gamekeepers who would chase off anyone bold enough to trespass. This situation was corrected following the Kinder Scout Trespass in 1932 and nowadays, as a result of the Countryside and Rights of Way Act 2000, all unimproved land above 1,000 feet is defined as 'open access land' in which public has the right to wander freely. That being said, these habitats are fragile, often containing rare plants and ground-nesting birds which are easily disturbed. Therefore people crossing these wild places, in particular with dogs, should be careful where they tread to avoid damage to wildlife or causing surface erosion.

Partially or fully sculpted mill stones can be found scattered over the area, left over from when Hathersage was a centre for quarrying the bedrock.

## Bradfield Dale

Bradfield is one of the largest parishes in England, situated in a lovely dale and extending over moor and agricultural land around the Damflask, Dale Dike, Strines, and Agden Reservoirs. As these supply much of Sheffield's water, the reservoirs and the streams that feed them must remain unpolluted, so Bradfield has been protected from development and has a low human population.

The twin settlements of High and Low Bradfield lie within the Peak District National Park and are unique in South Yorkshire in that they were never industrialised, so have retained their remote, rural character. High Bradfield is up on the hill, with its houses clustered around the church, built on the site of the old Norman castle. Low Bradfield rambles prettily along the River Loxley which is crossed at the village centre by a stone bridge.

**Left:** Looking north along Stanage Edge.
**Right:** Bradfield Dale and part of the Strines Reservoir. The Bradfield villages are further down the valley.

# Stocksbridge

Stocksbridge is the first industrial settlement on the River Little Don, which joins the main River Don further down the valley at Deepcar. This is one of the river valleys that were industrialised because of its water, and factories are still clustered along the dale floor with dwellings spreading up the steep southern slope. Stocksbridge is a steel town that was created by Samuel Fox in 1842 when he built a steel works, along with much of the town's infrastructure. In its time, it has been a very hard, gritty place, but these days the factories are cleaner, specialising in high quality products mainly for the aerospace industry so the air is clear, and care is taken that the water remains unpolluted.

Along with neighbouring Deepcar and Bolsterstone, Stocksbridge has a strong tradition for participating in brass bands and choral singing. The town's brass band is called 'Unite The Union', very much in step with its strong industrial worker roots.

The A616 Stocksbridge Bypass has gained notoriety as a haunted road with stories going back to the its construction in the 1980s of a variety of gruesome ghosts appearing, one of which scared the wits out of two policemen who left the force as a result.

**Above:** An original old rural cottage that has been preserved, just above Stocksbridge.

**Below:** Houses, including 'The Essence Of Beauty' salon, along Manchester Road in Stocksbridge.

**Opposite:** Looking down onto the Stocksbridge factories from a street higher up the dale side.

# West Yorkshire

The landscape of West Yorkshire is mostly industrial and urban, with towns that link and even merge through ribbon development that classically traced its main rivers, the Aire and the Calder. The heaviest industry is in the flatter south and east of the county, powered by coal from the mines around Wakefield, Castleford, Pontefract. The factories of Leeds, Huddersfield, Halifax and Bradford mostly grew around the wool and textile industries, which continue to this day alongside numerous new ventures born of Yorkshire ingenuity. Many of these businesses are housed in the old cotton and wool mill buildings, which remain sturdy and architecturally significant.

Industry followed the rivers and canals into the Pennine uplands where the precipitous streets of towns like Marsden, Hebden Bridge and Ripponden sit below the high fells. Housing and isolated mills are to be found on the moors above 1,000 feet making a unique and fascinating landscape where dwellings, industry, farming and boggy heather intertwine in surprising ways. So rows of houses tumble down steep slopes towards a factory chimney towering up above the trees in an otherwise quiet, pastoral valley. One great benefit is that the open splendour and isolation of the high Pennines is never far from even the most industrialised parts of Leeds or Halifax, and the moors can be readily accessed by dozens of footpaths that used to take workers from their rural homes to the factories. Indeed, it was the need for workers to travel to and from the mills that drove Parliament to act to formalise footpaths as legal rights of way. Access legislation has continued to evolve from the 18th century through to the 2000 Countryside and Rights of Way Act, providing immeasurable benefits to the entire population of Britain by opening the countryside to access on foot, cycle and horse.

**Below:** Holmfirth town centre with Holy Trinity Parish Church on the left. This attractive moor-side town lies south of Huddersfield on the River Holme. As well as textile industries, the town had stone and slate quarries, and more recently has become famous for being the location for the *Last of the Summer Wine* television series. The town also had a notoriety for its thriving saucy postcard factory that sadly closed in 2010.

# Industrial Heritage

The industrial heritage of West Yorkshire is to be found in its many mill buildings, foundries and mines, and in its transport network of roads, railways and canals. Heavy industry required the transport of coal, stone and steel from the mines and quarries to the mills, which would have been extremely difficult in the 18th and 19th centuries, before roads were paved. Initially, most transport was along rivers, which were not always navigable, prompting the construction of canals (or 'navigations') from the mid-18th century. The engineers would let nothing stand in their way as they pioneered routes for heavy cargoes across the Pennine Hills between the River Humber in the east to Lancashire in the west. These waterways had to climb hundreds of feet before traversing through long tunnels under the Pennine peaks and, as with all canals, had to be constantly fed with water to keep them open.

Canals in West Yorkshire include the Huddersfield Broad and Narrow canals, the Aire and Calder Navigation, the Bradford, and the Leeds and Liverpool, all of which are interconnected and link all of the main industrial centres. Their development meant that much higher tonnages of heavy materials could be moved, and far more reliably than before. However, their day came and went as the development of railways, sealed roads and the internal combustion engine allowed for greater speed, so they gradually fell into disuse. Today these great canals are devoted to leisure and tourism through boating and walking.

Many fine cotton and wool mill buildings remain which in the cases of Salts Mill in Saltaire and Lister Mill in Bradford still rank among the biggest buildings in Yorkshire. To gain a better understanding, there is a Yorkshire industrial heritage trail whose details can be found at http://www.makersminersmoney.org/.

**Right:** The Huddersfield Narrow Canal at Slaithwaite as it passes Slaithwaite Mills.

# Hebden Bridge

Hebden Bridge is another town that developed around the wool industry because it had the clean water and transport routes to the east and west which could support industrial weaving. This attractive town lies on the River Calder, high up in its valley and not far from the Pennine watershed. Its name derives from the bridge over the River Hebden, just before its confluence with the Calder, which enabled traffic to pass along the trans-pennine road without resorting to a ferry. Around 1800, one enterprising industrialist built the Gibson cotton mill high up in the valley of the Hebden (see pages 21 and 22). However the mill lost its business to more conveniently situated enterprises lower down the valley, near the Calder. When it closed in 1890, it became an 'Entertainment Emporium' thanks to its beautiful setting by the river, deep in its wooded valley and close to Hardcastle Crags. It is now a National Trust property with a museum, cafe and exhibitions.

The history of Hebden Bridge is industrial, but it now also fosters a culture of sustainability, supporting many small local businesses as well as an annual arts and blues festival.

**Page 20–21:** Scenes on the Rochdale Canal at Hebden Bridge and a stone stairway on the footpath to Hardcastle Crags.
**Page 22:** Gibson Mill by Hebden Water.
**Page 23:** Looking west to the moors above the Hebden valley.

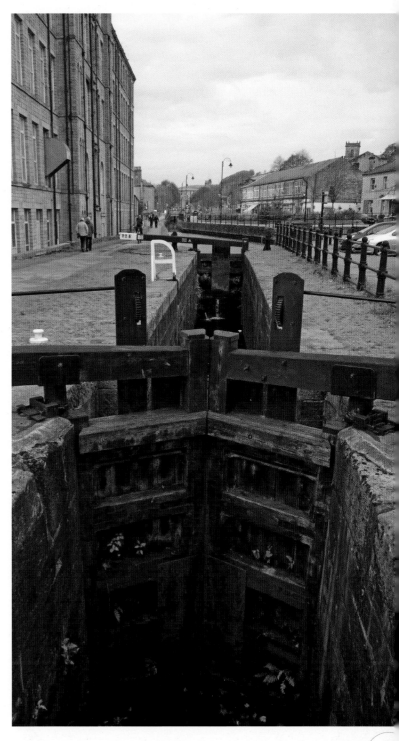

# Haworth and the Brontës

Haworth is another Pennine village with an industrial heritage, occupying both banks of the River Worth and climbing steeply up Haworth Moor. It is served by trains belonging to the Keighley and Worth Valley Railway heritage line that runs between Oxenhope and Keighley. The focus for tourists arriving at Haworth train station is the steep western half of the village, where the picturesque old Main Street climbs up the dale to the parish church of St Michael and All Angels. Patrick Brontë became the vicar in 1820, living in the parsonage which lies just across the graveyard and it was here that the Brontë sisters, Charlotte, Emily and Anne, lived for most of their lives. The village, as described by the Brontë Society, would have looked very different at that time:

> "The village where the Brontë sisters grew up was then a crowded industrial town, polluted, smelly and wretchedly unhygienic. Although perched on the edge of open country, high up on the edge of Haworth Moor, the death rate was as high as anything in London or Bradford, with 41 per cent of children failing even to reach their sixth birthday. The average age of death was just 24." (https://www.bronte.org.uk/)

The industrial revolution paved the way for the long and comfortable lives we live today, but it was a hard road for most people, including children, who had to work long gruelling days to earn enough to survive. Haworth lies above the 500 foot contour where the cool, damp climate, combined with the harsh living conditions, was a breeding ground for the tuberculosis that killed many, including Charlotte, Emily and Anne Brontë. Although life was more comfortable for a parson's family than for a mill worker, all of Patrick Brontë's children predeceased him, the longest-living being Charlotte, who died in her thirties.

Nowadays, however, Main Street and the surrounding area are odour free and delightful to explore, with trails that visit the church and the museum, and which climb through the lanes onto the open moors. The more energetic can follow trails over Penistone Hill and up to the Brontë Waterfalls, high on Haworth Moor.

**Left:** The parish church of St Michael and All Angels.
**Right:** Main Street, Haworth.

**Page 26:** Old Bingley on the River Aire with All Saints Parish Church. This photograph is taken from the bridge, which is high above the river, but was almost inundated when the river flooded during the winter of 2015. It rose rapidly until it broke its banks and flooded the ground floors of most of the buildings shown here, along with much of the town and surrounding countryside.

**Page 27:** Holmfirth, with Holy Trinity church tower in the foreground and Meltham Moor on the horizon.

## Halifax and the Calder Valley Towns

The minster town of Halifax lies above the larger Huddersfield in the Calder Valley. Both are market towns which grew around the still-thriving textile industry, starting with native wool and later processing imported cotton. In the 19th century, the town grew rapidly owing to the introduction of steam power, and by 1850 there were 24 mills in the town. The Dean Clough textile mill at more than half-a-mile long is one of the largest factory buildings in the country and now contains a hotel, retail centre and a theatre. Other Halifax industries over the years include Mackintosh's chocolate (Rolo and Quality Street), Timothy Taylor's brewery, Crossley Carpets and banking.

## Sport in Yorkshire

As far as cricket is concerned, Yorkshire is a single county, whose county cricket club, formed in 1863, has won more County Championship titles than any other. Because of strong participation at all levels, Yorkshire continues to produce many of England's most famous cricketers. The county ground is at Headingley in Leeds, but there are dozens of smaller grounds throughout Yorkshire, among which is the Wakefield St Michael's ground opposite with its lovely view over the city.

Yorkshire has a strong tradition in football, with top clubs based in Sheffield, Leeds, Huddersfield, Bradford, York and Hull; West Yorkshire is also at the centre of English rugby league, which has a reputation (disputed) for being even harder than the rugby union played elsewhere in England.

In recent times, Yorkshire has also taken cycling to its heart, particularly since 2015 when several stages of the Tour de France were staged in the county and, as part of the celebrations, yellow painted bicycles appeared in villages and on roads along the route. These now decorate the route of the annual Tour de Yorkshire cycle race.

**Above:** The town of Halifax in the Calder Valley.
**Right:** Wakefield St Michael's Cricket Ground with the towers of Wakefield on the skyline.

The view from the crags on Ilkley Moor on a day when a hat wasn't necessary (On Ilkley Moor Baht' 'At), with the town of Ilkley spreading along Wharfedale.

**Page 32:** The view over Wharfedale from above Otley.

**Page 33:** Small Yorkshire businesses (*Clockwise from the top left*):
Plants on sale outside a house in Sutton-on-the-Forest, North Yorkshire.
An old curiosity shop in Hawes, North Yorkshire.
Mrs Beighton's Sweet Shop at the top of Main Street, Haworth.
Inside the Green Dragon Inn at Hardraw, which provides access to Hardraw Force waterfall for a small fee.

# North Yorkshire: The Dales

The Yorkshire Dales National Park extends over an area of 1,770 square kilometres (680 square miles) of limestone hills, covering most of north-west Yorkshire. There are no big towns, and most settlements are well separated and of great local character, without mills and industrial clutter. The land is mostly used for sheep farming, interspersed with cattle and arable in the more fertile areas.

The Dales contain much of the finest limestone scenery in the UK, with glacier-cut valleys, limestone pavements and crags, and stone-built settlements that merge with the landscape. Each valley or 'dale' has its own distinctive character, shaped over thousands of years by the people who have lived and worked there: building the dry-stone walls, stone barns and flower-rich hay meadows. There are also spectacular waterfalls, sparkling rivers and becks (streams), and ancient broadleaved woodlands to be explored. The area does possess some industrial heritage which can be found in the scattered remains of former mine workings and other rural industries high up on the moors.

Limestone is fine-grained grey rock comprised mostly of the chalky shells of marine organisms that sunk to the bottom of a shallow sea around 300 million years ago. The rock is mostly a form of calcium carbonate that dissolves slowly in water, creating cracks that, over millions of years, grow into caverns. Water flows down through these cracks, taking the soil with it, eventually creating areas of exposed rock which can become very extensive. Examples of this can be seen at Malham Cove, in the Ribble Valley, and around Ingleton.

It is fantastic country for ramblers, cyclists and climbers who can roam its lanes and byways, but there is also a world to explore underground. The Dales are riddled with caves and potholes which are a magnet for speleologists who can access the vast network through many entrances scattered over the hills. Squeezing through 'The Cheese Press' in the damp darkness underground may not seem like fun to most, but the adventure of exploring this hidden world attracts hundreds of devotees and guided pot-holing for beginners is available in towns like Settle and Ingleton.

The Yorkshire Dales are intriguing and accessible, and a landscape where every bend and summit reveals another ravishing view, beckoning the visitor on to discover more.

**Left:** The upper reaches of Arkengarthdale at Langthwaite.
**Right:** Overlooking Malham Tarn. The wood and marsh are owned by the National Trust wildlife study centre whose building is just out of the picture.

# Malham, and the Mystery of Malham Cove

Malham is a small village surrounded by spectacular Dales countryside at the source of the River Aire. Although it is high and quite remote, people have lived here for a long time and traces of Iron Age boundaries and Bronze Age hunting are still to be found. The economy has always been rural, although a couple of small cotton mills provided employment during the 19th century, but they were too remote, so industry never got a foothold. Malham is exceptionally picturesque, with the young river running through the middle of the village, crossed by stone bridges and the green dales rising to the heights on either side. Sitting on its banks after a day's walk, enjoying a drink while the birds sing is hard to beat.

## Malham's Waterways

As has been said, rainwater slowly dissolves limestone, forming cracks and caverns, and doing very surprising things to waterways. A stream, which must be one of the shortest in England, flows out of Malham Tarn (previous page) and runs for less than a kilometre before entirely disappearing down a crack in the rocky surface. 1.6 kms to the south lies Malham Cove, which was formed by a large ice-age river that fell 80 m (260 ft), eroding the limestone to form this spectacular cliff. The river flow decreased over the centuries as its water found other routes, until the Cove became a dry cliff. (Although, exceptionally, a waterfall reappeared for the first time in centuries in December 2015 following the extremely high rainfall that flooded much of north-west England.)

Malham Beck emerges from a cave at the bottom of the Cove, but this stream is NOT directly connected to the one leaving the Tarn above. So it seems that streams cross each other at different levels inside the cave system lying behind the cliff. Cavers continue to explore the system in an effort to solve the mystery of where the water goes on its journey.

Malham Beck is joined by Gordale Beck at Malham to form the River Aire, which flows south through Skipton to Leeds, before emptying into the Ouse at Goole, at the opposite end of the county. A steep climb up Gordale Beck from Malham is rewarded with waterfalls and the spectacular limestone formations of Gordale Scar.

The vertical scale of the Malham Cove cliff can be judged from the image on the right where two climbers look like ants on the overhanging cliff face. Surprisingly, there are over 250 recognised climbing routes up the Cove, and climbers regularly reach the top without falling off!

**Left:** Limestone-walled fields rising from Malham village.
**Right:** Malham Cove with climbers.

# The Ribble Valley

The River Ribble starts at Ribble Head, which is the spectacular location of the Ribblehead Railway Viaduct (see page 41), although its actual source is a little further up the dale at Gayle Moor. The Viaduct was built in the 1870s as an alternative north–south railway route by over a thousand men who lived along with their families in temporary villages nearby. It is 440 yards (400 m) long and 104 feet (32 m) above the valley floor, carrying the Settle to Carlisle railway line over the boggy solitude of Batty Moss.

The viaduct lies in the midst of The Three Peaks, which are Whernside (page 51) to the north, Ingleborough (page 47) to the south-west and Pen-y-Ghent (page 40) to the south-east. Climbing all three of these in a single day is one of the most popular challenges in England, involving a 25 mile walk and 5,000 feet of ascent. This is quite an achievement in a single day, although as Alfred Wainright pointed out, the countryside is so beautiful and full of interest that cramming too much into one day seems to be missing the point somewhat.

The River Ribble flows south between the slopes of Ingleborough and Pen-y-Ghent, through a limestone landscape where strangely-shaped pale grey rocks stick up in the middle of the grassy fields, and huge cliffs line the valley in which are found the entrances to potholes and caverns. The village of Horton-in-Ribbleside (page 40) lies halfway down the dale, and is a favourite starting point for the many hikers and cavers. The river tumbles down a small waterfall below the village where, in the autumn, salmon can be seen leaping towards their spawning grounds in the high fells. The image opposite shows a group of photographers by the river at Horton, waiting to catch the migrating fish on their cameras as they leap through the air.

This is a watershed, so the River Ribble flows down between the attractive town of Settle and Giggleswick village and then heads west to Preston and the Atlantic coast; while just a few miles away, the River Aire flows east.

**Below:** Settle Market Place and the Olde Naked Man Cafe, which is reputed to be the oldest cafe in England. The market is open on Tuesdays and, like the town shops, is known for its local produce.

**Right:** Photographers waiting for salmon to leap on the River Ribble at Horton.

**Page 40:** St Oswald's Church at Horton-in-Ribblesdale with Pen-y-Ghent in the distance.
**Page 41:** The Ribblehead Viaduct from the floor of Batty Moss.

# Ingleton and the Falls

Whernside is a lozenge-shaped mountain that points roughly north–south between Dentdale and Ingleton in the western Dales. The plentiful rainfall runs off its slopes into the River Twiss to the west and the River Doe to the east, and the two rivers meet at Ingleton, becoming the River Greta. During the final couple of miles, they both descend about 500 feet, carving out deep valleys containing a series of waterfalls. The largest of these is Thornton Force (opposite), but there are many more that can be admired from the Ingleton Falls trail. This is a 4-mile circular walking route starting in the town and following both streams through their spectacular gorges. (The Trail is privately owned with tickets and parking available from the visitor centre. http://www.ingletonwaterfallstrail.co.uk/). Walkers will encounter lots of wildlife along the trail, including dippers (right), grey wagtails, orchids and many other wildflowers such as wild garlic (below).

Lying, as it does, at the foot of the largest hills in the Dales, Ingleton is a favourite centre for walkers, climbers and cavers. This is possibly the best area for caves in the country so the town offers guides who take groups to explore the easier passages with their huge chambers, stalactites and waterfalls.

Ingleton has a viaduct that used to link two train stations operated by competing companies that refused to link their lines. This meant that passengers were forced to walk to the other terminus and change trains before proceeding north or south. The line was finally closed in 1953 making the viaduct redundant.

**Right:** A Dipper taking a rest on the River Doe.
**Below:** Wild garlic flowering in a wood at Ingleton.
**Opposite:** Thornton Force on the River Twiss.

# Limestone Pavements

One of the most distinctive landscape features of the Yorkshire Dales National Park is the spectacular 'karst' scenery, where the exposed limestone produces some very curious and unusual formations. The most characteristic of these is limestone pavement (see below), made up of blocks, called clints, bounded by deep vertical fissures known as grikes. These formed beneath soil and vegetation, but over thousands of years, the slightly acid water found vertical lines of weakness in the rock, dissolving the limestone and widening the cracks into deep gullies. This process can also leave sculptural lumps of limestone projecting up through the soil, or large boulders sitting on the surface called 'erratics' (see page 47). In extreme cases, all of the soil may wash away leaving a stony limestone desert such as can be found on the western flanks of Ingleborough.

The deep fissures, or grikes, often contain some soil in which a rich diversity of plants grows, kept moist and protected from wind and weather. Here are found liverworts and mosses, hart's tongue and maidenhair ferns, thyme, herb robert, speedwell, lily-of-the-valley and even stunted trees such as hawthorn and yew (see page 56), making peering down grikes something of a botanical adventure. Where surface soil has remained and the land has not been artificially fertilised, limestone grassland is a rich habitat for lime-loving wildflowers, including orchids that specialise in living on calcareous soils.

**Opposite:** A 'money tree' on the Ingleton Waterfall Trail. There are a few examples of these on the Trail, where thousands of coins have been hammered into fallen timber, in this case beside the River Twiss.

**Below:** Karst limestone that has been stripped of soil with wind-blown hawthorn trees managing to cling on in the harsh conditions.

**Page 46:** A limestone pavement on Twistleton Scar with Ingleborough on the horizon.
**Page 47:** An 'erratic' (exposed limestone boulder) on the west side of Twistleton Dale with the bulk of Ingleborough to the east.

# The Northern Dales

North of Ribblehead and Ingleborough, the karst ends and the landscape reverts to steep-sided hills capped by miles of open moor and blanket peat. This north-western corner of Yorkshire is sparsely populated, so the only settlements to be found in the thirty miles between the Ribble Valley and Teesdale are the small town of Hawes, in Wensleydale, and the villages of Muker, Thwaite and Keld in the upper reaches of Swaledale.

The market town of Hawes – the name Hawes means a 'pass between mountains' – lies on Bale Beck where it joins the River Ure in Wensleydale. At 850 feet above sea level, it is the highest town in England, sustained by sheep farming, tourism and country pursuits such as shooting and fishing; a fact reflected in the range of shops in the town. Although the area is very rural, there is evidence of industrial activity, some of which is on display at Gayle Mill, in the centre of Hawes. This is an 18th century water-powered cotton spinning mill, which became a saw mill in the 19th century and is now a tourist attraction.

The Pennine Way is probably the most famous long-distance walking route in England, starting at Edale in the Derbyshire Peaks and running 268 miles to Kirk Yetholme in the Scottish Borders. It passes through Hawes, before ascending to 2350 feet (716 m) on the massive limestone ridge of Great Shunner Fell. From this rugged mossy summit, the Way plunges into the verdant pastures of Wensleydale where sheep farming and wool have always been the mainstays of the community. It then follows the River Swale north before climbing once more towards the Tan Hill Inn (opposite), which is the highest pub in England at 1,732 feet (528 m). The Inn was established in the 18th century to serve the adjacent lead mines but now thrives on the custom of long-distance walkers and tourists. The snow vehicle (opposite) was bought some time ago from an Antarctic expedition to ferry people on and off the mountains when the inn is snow-bound and it is still in use today. This is Yorkshire's most north-westerly corner from which you can see far into Cumbria to the north-west and Teesdale to the north-east.

Wildlife seems to be relatively unafraid of humans in this remote spot, so curlews, lapwings and black grouse are often to be seen foraging very close to the Inn.

**Opposite:** The Pennine Way approaching the Tan Hill from the south.
**Right:** The polar vehicle at the Tan Hill Inn.

**Page 50:** Sunlit fields near Wath in Nidderdale.
**Page 51:** Upper Wensleydale at Hardraw with Great Whernside on the horizon.

# Arkengarthdale and Swaledale

Arkengarthdale is the most northerly dale in Yorkshire. Strung along Arkle Beck are the wonderfully-named settlements of Foggergill, Whaw, Booze and Arkle Town, which isn't a town at all, but a few houses climbing the dale side up a steep lane. Langthwaite is the largest settlement, boasting a Parish Church, a school and a pub nestling beside the beck. The village and its arched stone bridge were featured in the TV series *All Creatures Great and Small* about a Dales vet. Arkle Beck winds its way south-west through its lonely, beautiful valley, collecting water from dozens of smaller streams that tumble steeply down the glacier-cut valley sides from the high fells. Seeing the gentle pace of life now, it is hard to imagine that people used to earn a meagre living mining the hard rock in all weathers.

The small market town of Reeth lies on a relatively level sward at the confluence of Arkle Beck and the River Swale and has held a market on its broad village green (see below) for centuries. It was once a commercial centre for lead-mining as well as wool, so is well supplied with pubs and hotels. In recent times, Reeth has become a local centre for arts and crafts.

Swaledale (see page 54) runs in an easterly direction to Richmond (page 55), where the dales subside into the North Yorkshire plains. It is another glacier-cut limestone dale, with steep sides and broad valley bottom, where sheep graze in green meadows bounded by dry stone walls. Several projects to improve biodiversity in the area are underway, including the re-introduction of the practice of mowing meadows after the wild flowers have dropped their seeds to encourage diversity. A summer stroll through such places is rewarded by bands of bright colour from an astonishing variety of flowers where birds and butterflies thrive.

The town of Richmond was founded in 1071, when William the Conqueror granted lands to Alan Rufus as a reward for services. Rufus built Richmond Castle overlooking the Swale whose keep and walls still encompass the town's extensive market place. Richmond is now an important regional centre that also serves the huge army garrison of Catterick.

**Left:**  Upper Arkengarthdale and the Whaw village.
**Below:**  Reeth market place on market day.

**Page 54:**  Swaledale from near Marrick.
**Page 55:**  The town of Richmond with its Norman keep rising above the River Swale.

# Central North Yorkshire

Between the Dales in the west and the Yorkshire Moors in the east, the central part of North Yorkshire is a lower-lying landscape, undulating gently between rivers and streams. There are plenty of towns and villages, the largest being York. The valley is the main transport corridor between the north-east and southern England and accommodates the A1, along with many other main roads, the main East Coast Railway line, canals and major rivers. There is little heavy industry, but the fertile land, combined with the canny Yorkshire flair for business, has made the area quite prosperous.

Although the valley is scenically less spectacular than the Pennines and Moors, many of the numerous villages and towns straddling its highways are full of character and culturally rich. There are two cathedral cities: York with its Minster is the seat of England's second-highest ranking archbishop, and Ripon is one of the smallest cathedral cities in the country, but also boasts a nearby World Heritage Site at Fountains Abbey and Studley Park.

Because this valley has always been the main north–south corridor, it is of great strategic importance and has seen many major battles, some of which determined the future of England. These include the battle of Stamford Bridge, in which King Harold defeated the Danes immediately before hurrying south to die in the Battle of Hastings; and Marston Moor during the Civil War when the Royalists lost the North of England to Oliver Cromwell. Castles are to be found at Richmond, York, Knaresborough, Ripley and Bolton.

For sporting enthusiasts, there are racecourses at York, Wetherby, Thirsk and Ripon, while cricket, football and rugby grounds are to be found in most towns and many villages.

**Below:** The rich vale of York between Thirsk and York viewed from Crayke.

**Opposite** (*clockwise from the top left*): A Lapwing, photographed by the Tan Hill Inn; A Meadow Pipit on Stanton Moor, near Holmfirth; A tree attempting to grow in a limestone grike in the Dales; Early Purple Orchids above Ingleton.

**Page 58:** Stillington Village.
**Page 59:** Easingwold Market Place and war memorial.

# York

During the first century AD, the Romans built a fortress called Eboracum on the site of the present Minster, close to the confluence of the rivers Ouse and Foss. Because of its strategic position in its fertile valley between the Moors and the Pennines, with the Great North Road and two large rivers for transport, York was often under siege. It has been successively occupied by the Romans, the Saxons, the Vikings, who called it Jorvik, and the Normans, each conqueror in turn using it as a regional capital. So York's castles and churches have been repeatedly destroyed and rebuilt with each war up to the 17th century.

Work on building York Minster was started by the Normans in 1080, but the main gothic structure was added in the 13th century in an effort to match Canterbury Cathedral, making it one of the largest cathedrals of its kind, dominating the city centre. The beautiful Cathedral Precinct contains a number of interesting and historic buildings, such as the ecclesiastical college, the Treasurer's House (managed by the National Trust), the library, and the remains of ancient cloisters (right).

York retains its Norman castle keep, along with the most complete city walls in England, partly dating from Roman times. These encircle the old city with its many churches, museums and the well-preserved medieval Shambles (page 62), where timber-framed 15th century buildings overhang the narrow streets. Museums include the Jorvik Viking Centre and the National Railway Museum.

Today, with its university, cathedral and vibrant city centre, York continues to be a strong regional centre for commerce, culture, the church and tourism.

# Knaresborough

Knaresborough lies on the winding River Nidd between Harrogate and York. During Henry II's reign, its 12th century castle was owned by Hugh de Morville who led the group that murdered Archbishop Thomas Becket at Canterbury Cathedral in 1170. Since then, the castle has been repeatedly besieged owing to its strategic position, so it is far from complete. The town has a few curiosities, such as the troglodyte house underneath the castle, and Mother Shipton's Cave, which is said to have been charging for entrance longer than any other tourist attraction in Britain.

Knaresborough has a weekly market that has taken place since the 14th century, and has a lively culture, holding an annual summer arts festival.

**Opposite:** The railway viaduct crosses the River Nidd at Knaresborough.
**Right:** People relax in the peaceful York Minster precinct alongside the ancient cloisters.

**Page 62:** The Shambles Market in central York.
**Page 63:** York Minster and the city's roofs and steeples from York Castle.

# The Howardian Hills

East of York City, the land rises towards the gentle Howardian Hills. This ridge runs north-west from Kirkham Priory and the River Derwent to Helmsley, on the edge of the North York Moors National Park. It is a well-wooded rolling countryside containing a patchwork of arable and pasture fields and scenic villages. The landscape has been largely moulded by the owners of the historic country houses lying within the Howardian Hills Area of Outstanding Natural Beauty, including Castle Howard, Hovingham Hall and others, each with its landscaped park.

Coxwold (see opposite) is a pretty Howardian village of stone houses that line a wide street containing the Fauconberg Arms Inn and the large Parish Church of St Michael with its octagonal tower. Below the ridge to the north of Coxwold lie the ruins of Byland Abbey which was founded in the 12th century by Savigniac monks but, like nearby Rievaulx, was destroyed in the Reformation. The Kilburn White Horse can be seen on the right edge of the picture: it is the most northerly turf-cut figure in Britain, dating from 1857, when the outline of the horse was originally marked out by the Kilburn village schoolmaster and his pupils.

## Game Birds and Shooting

The Shooting UK web site says: "The vast county of Yorkshire with its varied landscape contains hundreds of good shoots..." and goes on to list the biggest and best of these. On the plains, the quarry is pheasant and partridge, while on the moors, the choice bird is grouse, and each year, millions of game birds are raised for the sole purpose of being shot. The lucrative and somewhat exclusive sports of hunting, shooting and fishing are greatly enjoyed by certain people and they also motivate landowners to preserve woods and scrub that might otherwise be cleared. Landowners also try to ensure that rivers are maintained well to support trout and salmon. There is no doubt that everyone benefits from the large areas of Britain that look more varied and natural because of country sports, but there is a downside: other wild animals, such as raptors, weasels and stoats, jackdaws and jays, are often killed because they could threaten the health of game bird populations. In addition, practices like the regular burning of heather on the moors for the benefit of grouse endanger the habitats of the natural inhabitants.

Across this over-crowded island many competing interests operate, and whether something is 'good' or 'bad' often depends upon the perspective of the observer. In these Yorkshire hills, one can be grateful for the beauty of this highly-managed landscape, and also for the colour that the game birds bring to the fields and woods, but many are alarmed at the decline of native wildlife.

**Opposite:** View over Coxwold towards the white horse carved into the southern edge of the North Yorkshire Moors above the village of Kilburn. Sutton Bank is just on the other side of the ridge.

**Right:** Game cocks in their spring plumage. Left: A Black Grouse; Right: A Red-legged Partridge; Bottom: A Pheasant.

# The North Yorkshire Moors

The North Yorkshire Moors cover a sandstone plateau that rises steeply up from the Plain of York and extends 30 miles eastward to the North Sea coastal cliffs. The rounded heights, covered in peat bog and heather, rise to 454 metres (1485 feet) at Urra Moor, but are cut into by deep wooded valleys which are mostly farmed. The largest valley is Eskdale, whose River Esk starts in the high Cleveland Hills in the western part of the moors and flows east all the way to Whitby on the spectacular North Sea Coast. On a dull day, the moors can be very bleak and seem to stretch endlessly to a blurry horizon, but in reality this national park contains quite a variety of landscapes and charming corners. There are many wonderful views, such as that from the summit of Sutton Bank in the west (page 68), and the North Sea cliff in the east. The Moors towns of Helmsley, Kirkbymoorside and Pickering along the southern edge are full of character and there are a number of pretty villages in unique valley settings. Then there are ruined abbeys at Rievaulx, Byland and Whitby, a heritage railway, wildlife refuges and lots of opportunities for grouse shooting in the many estates across the Moors.

Today, the Moors are popular, not only for hiking, cycling and other outdoor pursuits, but also with people who just want to admire the beautiful scenery from a car; or from the North Yorkshire Moors Railway whose line crosses the high moors between Pickering and Whitby, pulled by the Royal Scot and other heritage steam locomotives (page 80).

Before the days of tourism, mining supplemented agriculture to sustain the communities. In the 19th century iron mining and processing boomed, as ironstone mines were opened in many locations. One such is peaceful Rosedale (below), where a railway was built around the top of the dale to serve the mines and kilns were constructed to process the ore. Low-grade coal was also dug up to feed the kilns for nearly 200 years until the early 20th century. The hikers in the image below are walking on the route of the old railway track.

A lot of mining activity is evident along the North Sea coast, where alum was mined for fixing textile dyes and a working potash mine still exists at Boulby, on the edge of the Moors. Gem quality jet has always been found in the area, becoming particularly popular in the 19th century when it was fashionable for jewellery. Today jet items can be bought in shops in the region, particularly in the old part of Whitby.

**Below:**  Hikers setting out on the trail around Upper Rosedale which was once the railway line.
**Opposite:**  Bransdale, looking towards Cockayne, high in the Moors above Kirkbymoorside.

**Page 68:**  The view from the top of Sutton Bank on a winter's day.
**Page 69:**  Wintry moors near Gillamoor.

# Helmsley

The elegant town of Helmsley is cradled by hills at the end of Rye Dale, on the south-western edge of the Moors. It is a small town of handsome sandstone buildings centred around the big market square (left) with its gothic Victorian Feversham monument. Helmsley has long been a stopping point on the main road to Scarborough, and consequently has four coaching inns and a number of cafes, restaurants and food shops on the square. The Arts Centre and shops selling country goods, antiques and books are to be found on the surrounding streets, one of which leads to the 12th century castle with its impressive surviving tower.

Close by the town is the 3,000 acre Duncombe Park with its 200-room 18th century house that is still the home of the Fevershams. The park has a rich and rare ecosystem that includes a National Nature Reserve containing some of the oldest and tallest native trees in the country: a remnant of the ancient forests that once covered much of England.

# North Yorkshire Abbeys

A number of small abbeys and priories existed in Yorkshire from Saxon times, but the great era of monastic building was in the 12th century, when Byland (pictured on the right), Coverham, Easby, Fors, Fountains, Hood, Jervaulx and Rievaulx Abbeys were built by Cistercian (including Savignac) and Benedictine orders. Monks from France were joined by those from the smaller Yorkshire priories, which were then dissolved. The churches were magnificent edifices signifying the greatness of God, with substantial buildings attached to house the monks and the lay-brothers (who did most of the manual work). Many of the abbeys became wealthy and locally powerful, but all were dissolved and partially dismantled during the Reformation between 1530–1539. Their wealth was taken by the King's exchequer and the buildings and land were sold or given by Henry VIII to favoured nobles.

The Cistercian abbeys of Byland and Rievaulx, both curated today by English Heritage, lie only 7 miles (10 kms) apart: the former just below the southern edge of the Yorkshire Moors and Rievaulx deep in Rye Dale.

# Kirkbymoorside

Kirkbymoorside lies a few miles east of Helmsley on the southern edge of the Moors. It has been a market town since the middle ages and has two ancient coaching inns, the Black Swan with its carved porch, and the timber-framed George and Dragon.

In a dale above Kirkbymoorside sits the picturesque village of Hutton-le-Hole. There is something other-worldly in the way its pretty houses are arranged on either bank of Hutton Beck, flowing in a wide grassy valley through the middle of the village. Hutton is a very popular destination, particularly in the summer when the Rydale Folk Museum is open. This comprises a six-acre site containing historic buildings, livestock, and live demonstrations of traditional hand crafts and farming practices.

**Opposite:** A January dawn in Helmsley Market Place with the Feversham Monument.
**Right:** Byland Abbey.

**Page 72:** Kirkbymoorside Market Place.
**Page 73:** Hutton-le-Hole on a spring evening.

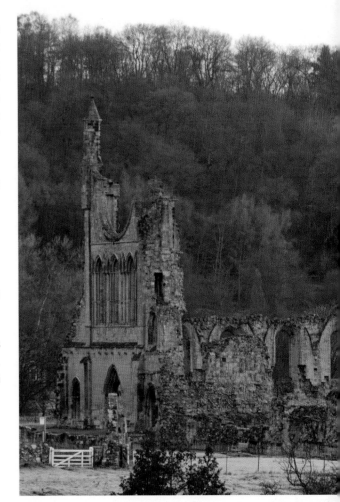

## Rosedale, Ironstone Mines and the Trackway

Today, the little village of Rosedale Abbey is a quiet rural community with just a few walkers and a minor road junction to disturb the peace. In the latter half of the 19th century, however, it was the centre of a flourishing iron-mining industry, because of a valuable seam of ironstone that lies beneath the surface. Higher up Rosedale, shafts were sunk and huge red sandstone kilns were built to roast the ore. In order to transport the resulting pig-iron out, the North Yorkshire and Cleveland Railway Company extended its line to run around the head of Rosedale, requiring the trains to climb a 1 in 5 gradient on the Ingleby Incline.

The mines operated for about 50 years, and what remain are the old track-way around the top of Rosedale and the ruins of some buildings and kilns. Today this is a bridle path offering a delightful stroll surrounded by heather where grouse can be seen, and it is hard to imagine how grim it must have been with the dust and smoke from the kilns and trains when the mines were working.

**Left:** The remains of the kilns which roasted the ore from the Rosedale East Mines until 1911.
**Above:** Rosedale with the village of Rosedale Abbey.

**Page 76:** The moors at Lowna on the River Dove, above Kirkbymoorside.
• **Page 77:** Roseberry Topping on a crisp spring morning, with smoke rising from the industrial chimneys of Middlesborough in the background.

## The Top of the Yorkshire Moors: Heather and the Big Sky

There are no settlements on the bleak and wind-swept tops of the Yorkshire Moors, where the rounded, peaty tops rise well above 1,000 feet to the highest point at Urra Moor (454 m or 1490 ft). However, the climate here is actually somewhat better than in the Pennines in whose rain shadow the Moors lie. The ubiquitous heather is perfect for grouse and other game birds and is periodically burned as part of the shooting business, to promote the growth of young shoots upon which the grouse feed. This explains the oblong patches of heather, alternatively short or tall, that can be seen where shooting takes place, indicating that this is far from being a natural landscape, but one that is closely managed for an economic purpose.

Few roads cross the moors, but there are numerous tracks, some of which are ancient ways or Roman roads and others for shooting access. It is a big space in which to roam, contrasting sharply with the varied appeal of the deep green dales dotted with farms, woods and the odd village.

**Above:** A post on the high moors, probably signalling a land boundary.
**Left:** A meadow pipit on a frosty morning.
**Opposite:** Hiking up Simon Howe Rigg on a damp day. Beside the cairn at the summit are Bronze Age standing stones.

**Opposite:** Goathland Station on the North Yorkshire Moors Railway line that runs from Pickering to Grosmont and Whitby. The line fell victim to the Beeching railway consolidation in 1965 but, following years of hard effort by local enthusiasts, was reopened as far as Grosmont in 1975. The company is still mostly run by volunteers but provides a timetabled daily service for the public, often using heritage locomotives.

**Above:** The sculpture of a young and handsome Captain James Cook at Great Ayton, facing east towards Staithes, where his interest in the sea started. Cook went to the school in Great Ayton for eight years from the age of eight and the building is now a museum in his memory. At the time of this photograph, he is being pursued by a wooden sculpture of a British soldier erected on the centenary of the start of World War One.

**Right:** The Captain Cook Monument on its Cleveland Hills ridge above Great Ayton.

# The East Coast

### The True Extent of Yorkshire?

When is a county not a county? When it's a unitary authority, in this case Redcar and Cleveland. Until the 1972 Local Government Act abolished it, the North Riding of Yorkshire extended to the River Tees, as is still shown on some maps. However the county of North Yorkshire now ends at Staithes and has been placed in a different region (Yorkshire and Humberside) from the northerly area, which is now in the North-East Region. This was a deeply unpopular change at the time, and since the North Riding of Yorkshire existed for a long time beforehand, I have decided to include some of the glorious coastline just north of the present border in this book.

### The Cleveland Way and Saltburn

The Cleveland Way is a long-distance walking route starting at Helmsley and following the Cleveland Hills northward on the west side of the Moors, then turning east, leaving the National Park at Guisborough and ending at Saltburn-by-the-Sea. This little resort town developed in the 19th century as a terminus of the Stockton & Darlington Railway which served the iron mines on the Moors. As the mining declined, an industrialist named Henry Pease, seeing Saltburn's potential as a seaside resort, built the Zetland Hotel with its own platform inside the hotel. The steep cliff was an obstacle to hotel guests wanting to enjoy the pier and beach below, so The Saltburn Cliff Lift was constructed in 1884 and is now one of the world's oldest water-powered funicular railways.

**Above:** This photograph was taken from the Cleveland Way, immediately above Saltburn-by-the-Sea, on the week that the closure of the Redcar Steel Works was announced. The smoke and steam in this picture will therefore no longer be seen rising, with major implications for unemployment in the area. The contrast between the rural beauty and calm on this cliff-top and the heavy industry just to the north is stark, but quite typical along this coast.

**Opposite:** The Cleveland Way at Hummersea. The Way follows the coastline, climbing the huge cliffs that rise to well over 500 feet and occasionally dipping down to sea level, encountering plenty of industrial heritage in the valleys and scattered among the fields and along the cliffs and shoreline. There are extensive abandoned alum and iron mines and a large operational potash works at Boulby. However the countryside is rural and the views along the cliffs are quite spectacular, so the walk contains an ideal combination of beauty and features of interest.

## Staithes

Staithes is the most north-easterly point of the present county of North Yorkshire, separated from Redcar and Cleveland by Staithes Beck. It is very compact, with cottages on narrow lanes descending the steep slopes to a harbour, protected by the cliffs and two long breakwaters. These have served the village well as the harbour remains intact, whereas at some other ports on this coast, harbour walls and breakwaters have been completely destroyed by storms. Staithes was once an important port for fishing and for international trade and had a railway station until 1958. Today, fishing boats still use the harbour, but the village relies mostly on tourism.

During the early 20th century, Staithes was home to a group of artists known as the "Northern Impressionists", who were inspired to set up their own artists' colony, having worked in similar groups in France.

On leaving school in Great Ayton (see page 81), the youthful Captain James Cook took up employment as an apprentice in a grocer's shop in Staithes, but it was not a success and within two years he moved to Whitby. There he was apprenticed to a shipping company, learning seamanship on coal coasters plying to and from the south.

The area around Staithes is geologically interesting for its minerals (iron ore, potash and alum) that spawned the mines and quarries along this coast; and for the huge Jurassic cliffs which reveal geological history, including dinosaur fossils, embedded in the strata.

**Above:** Approaching Staithes along the Cleveland Way from the north.
**Opposite:** Staithes Beck at low tide with the town rising behind it. The harbour is cradled in the gap between the cliffs to the left and right.

## Whitby

A settlement has existed where Whitby lies on the Esk estuary since the Dark Ages and the first abbey was founded in 650 by the Christian King Oswy of Northumbria under the abbess Hilda. The monastery was destroyed in 867 by Viking raiders, replaced in 1078, then finally dissolved at the time of the reformation. Today its ruins can be found spectacularly situated on the East Cliff, where they are open to the public, managed by English Heritage.

Fishing has always taken place here but the town also developed from the 18th century as a port and centre for shipbuilding and whaling, as well as trading in locally mined alum and Whitby jet jewellery. From the 19th century, it has also become a very popular tourist destination because of its location, the abbey and its busy harbour. The town climbs steeply up towards the moors, which can be accessed by walkers, or for the less energetic, the North Yorkshire Moors Railway runs day trips over the moors to Pickering from the train station.

## Scarborough

There is a story that Scarborough was founded in the 10th century by a Viking called Thorgils Skarthi, who called the settlement *Skarðaborg*. However, there is no archaeological evidence for this and little is recorded in the Domesday Book. Actually, it may be safe to assume that its origins are considerably earlier and that the history was lost during constant raids from the sea. Henry II built the castle on the strategically important headland overlooking the harbour and it was added to by succeeding monarchs. However a 5-month siege by Parliamentarians during the Civil War left the castle and town heavily damaged. During the ensuing centuries, a garrison was established at the castle. which was also used as a prison until, in 1914, German battleships attacked Scarborough, firing some 500 shells that again severely damaged the castle and town.

The railway brought tourism and the Grand Hotel was built, which stands out proudly above the North Bay (see above). Scarborough developed into a popular holiday destination and spa, and remains the largest holiday resort on the Yorkshire coast offering a striking setting, a good sandy bay, an active harbour, a theatre and lots of musical events during the year. Scarborough also has a famous cricket club hosting first class fixtures and producing many famous players, including W.G. Grace. Every August for over 130 years the club has hosted a cricketing and social festival, attracting many well-known faces.

**Opposite:**  Whitby seen from the main road bridge over the River Esk, with the abbey ruins on the right.
**Above:**  A girl enjoys the view from South Sands across Scarborough Bay to the Grand Hotel and the castle remains.

# Flamborough Head

Flamborough Head is a chalky peninsula that extends about 6 kilometres into the North Sea from the north end of Bridlington beach. It is now a very important conservation site for seabirds, but in the 19th century, people shot the birds for sport, and also to decorate ladies' hats. The population declined drastically until local MP Christopher Sykes successfully introduced the first Act in the United Kingdom to protect wild birds in 1869.

The Yorkshire Wildlife Trust now protects the cliffs where internationally important numbers of breeding seabirds, including fulmars, herring gulls, kittiwakes, guillemots, razorbills and puffins, are to be found. The cliff-top heaths with their chalk grasslands, rich in wildflowers including orchids, also host many land birds.

A stroll around the Head is rewarded by lots of wildlife and magnificent views under the soaring tower of the lighthouse.

**Opposite:** Flamborough Head Lighthouse.

**Inset:** Puffins on a grassy area near the cliff top.

**Right:** The Chalk Tower, which was built to be a lighthouse in the 18th century but was never used for that purpose.

**Page 90:** Looking down through the eroded chalk cliffs from the top of Flamborough Head.

**Page 91:** Guillemots, Razorbills and Gulls cling to the vertical cliffs, taking advantage of every crack and crevice.

# The Yorkshire Wolds

The Yorkshire Wolds are chalk hills that rise from the Vale of York to over 800 feet at their highest point, extending eastward to the North Sea cliffs at Flamborough Head. To the north is the Vale of Pickering and in the south is the River Humber whose valley divides the Yorkshire Wolds from a smaller range of chalk wolds in Lincolnshire. This is a gentle, rural landscape of unique character deriving from the form of the land, the lack of flowing water and the nature of the farms that cover it. The hills are rounded and divided by long glacial valleys winding sinuously through them, lending interesting shapes to the fields and the woodlands between. As in the limestone Dales, the apparent lack of streams is because they are underground, the water having dissolved the chalk, creating channels and cracks under the surface. So rain that lands on the Wolds seems to disappear, only to appear above ground as fully-fledged streams some distance away, where the hills meet the plains. This can be seen near Driffield where the River Hull seems to appear out of nowhere.

The charm of the Wolds was revealed to the World when David Hockney started painting them on returning to his childhood home in Bridlington. He captured the long views from the scarp at Garrowby in the west, the colours and forms of the valleys around Thixendale and the more subtle beauty to be found in the flatter east around Bridlington. Through his depictions of The Wolds, Hockney shows us the value of stopping and absorbing the colours and textures, even of unremarkable landscapes, at any time of year.

Travelling slowly is the best way to enjoy the Wolds and hikers have the Yorkshire Wolds Way, a long-distance walking route from the River Humber to Filey, while cyclists who don't mind some steep hills have plenty of quiet lanes to explore.

The Wolds can feel quite remote as they are sparsely populated and lack large villages and towns, so are a refuge from the industrial towns along the nearby River Humber.

**Opposite:**  The evening sun shines on the cliffs of Flamborough Head from Bridlington, contrasting with the dark groin on Bridlington Beach.
**Below:**  The Vale of Pickering retreating to the dark line of the Moors, viewed from Birdsall Brow at the northern edge of the Wolds.

**Page 94:**  Sheep graze peacefully in Water Dale, in the middle of the Wolds.
**Page 95:**  Cyclists climbing a steep lane from Thixendale.

Opposite: Birdsall House in the Wolds south of Norton-on-Derwent. It was built by the Sotheby family after the dissolution of the Monasteries in 1540 and has been owned by the Willoughby family since Thomas Willoughby married the heiress daughter in 1719. It is run as a farming and shooting estate.

Above: Fairy Dale, whose steep sides and wide bottom are typical of glacier-carved valleys. There are quarry workings and an abandoned railway in the upper reaches of the dale, but it is now an important conservation area as it is the home of many rare chalkland plants.

Right: South Dalton basks in warm summer sunshine.

Page 98: A lone hiker sets off across the snow from Settrington Beacon at the top of Thorpe Bassett Wold. The beacon could be seen over a wide area and was lit if the beacons at Scarborough and York were seen ablaze. The adjacent road has Roman origins and served this signal station for two thousand years, until 1931.

Page 99: Winter snow cloaks fields on Settrington Wold.

**Left:** The richly agricultural scarp at Uncleby Wold descends to the Vale of York.

**Above:** St Mary's Parish Church at Huggate whose tall spire was depicted in Hockney's paintings of the village.

**Right:** The Rudston Monolith. This was erected in about 1600 BC and is the tallest monolith in the United Kingdom at over 7.6 metres (25 ft), weighing about 26 tons. It is grey sandstone from Cayton Bay, about ten miles distant. Although it now lies in the churchyard of All Saints Parish Church at Rudston, the monolith existed here for nearly 3,000 years before the church was built. Throughout the world, sites of pagan religious significance have been converted to Christian churches and shrines.

## Holderness

During the ice ages, glaciers formed in the Wolds chalk, carving deep valleys and carrying countless tons of eroded rock fragments down to the frozen sea. As the ice melted, the fragments settled, forming new land comprised of a soft sedimentary rock. This new land is a low-lying plain stretching from Flamborough Head in the north down to Spurn Head on the Humber Estuary, and east to Beverley and Kingston-upon-Hull. These glacial deposits provide fertile soils that can support intensive arable cultivation in large fields which are generally bounded by drainage ditches rather than hedges. There is very little woodland and only a few knolls and small hills, which are high points in the underlying chalk poking through the plain. Consequently it is wide and somewhat featureless landscape.

One consequence of the softness of the sedimentary surface rock of Holderness is that the coastline suffers the highest rate of coastal erosion in Europe. This is exacerbated by the shape of the coastline and by increasingly severe storms at sea. Several feet of land are being lost each year, and a look at a map reveals that many roads end mysteriously at the cliff edge. The resulting silt is carried south and deposited elsewhere, notably around The Wash, where the coastline is gradually expanding. In relatively recent times a lot of silt was deposited at Spurn Head making it grow and seem permanent but, at the time of writing, the Head has been eroded to the extent that some sections are now extremely narrow and its paved road has disintegrated.

## Beverley

Beverley was once the tenth-largest town in England and very wealthy. Its riches came from wool produced by the fertile East Riding farms, and also from pilgrims who came to venerate its founding saint, John of Beverley. The pilgrimage business and resulting income were lost following the Reformation, resulting in a dramatic down-turn in the town's status from which it never entirely recovered. Today, however, it is an attractive market town with many historic buildings, a lively market, a thriving music scene, and a racecourse. Its most prominent landmark is Beverley Minster which, whilst larger than one third of English cathedrals, is nonetheless a parish church.

**Below:** Typical Holderness farmland to the east of Hull.
**Opposite:** An approach to Beverley Minster.

**Page 104:** The beach at Withernsea.
**Page 105:** The River Humber and the Humber Bridge from North Ferriby.

## The Humber Estuary

The River Humber is actually an estuary for its entire length, starting 7 miles (11 kms) east of Goole where the rivers Ouse and Trent merge, and flowing into the North Sea at Spurn Head, about 30 miles (50 kms) to the east. It is very broad, quite shallow and the deep silt in its bed moves about with the tides, so navigating large ships on it requires great expertise and local knowledge. Cargo ships come and go with goods from all parts of the world from its ports of Hull, Grimsby, Immingham, New Holland and North Killingholme.

The Humber was a major obstacle in the way of people and goods travelling by land up England's east coast until the construction of the 7,280 ft single span Humber Bridge that linked Lincolnshire to the East Riding of Yorkshire for the first time. Unfortunately it has been under-used since its opening, owing to the arrival of the M62 and the decline in industries requiring heavy transport, such as coal mining around Selby and fishing in Grimsby.

**Above:** Drax power station, between Goole and Selby, which burns mostly coal, alongside an array of wind turbines. Its generating capacity of 3,960 megawatts is the highest of any power station in the United Kingdom or Western Europe, supplying about 7% of the country's electricity. The Drax company are working to make the plant less polluting, so have installed advanced filters and other new equipment. They were also experimenting with carbon capture and storage until government support was reduced in 2015. At the time of writing, they are moving towards biomass, whose overall environmental benefits depend upon the source of the wood used and the cost of transport from the United States. Coal-fired power stations are being phased out so the cooling towers in this image are likely to disappear from the landscape within a decade or two.

**Opposite:** The M62 bridge over the River Ouse at Goole. The Ouse starts at the confluence of the rivers Swale and Ure north of York and joins the Humber a few miles beyond this bridge.

## Spurn Head

Spurn Head has probably existed since the ice ages, but is far from a permanent feature as it is moving west at a rate of about 2 metres per year. It is a dynamic piece of land, constantly being eroded by the sea at the same time as material from coastal erosion further north is being deposited. Spurn Head is about 3 miles long from Kilnsea to its southern tip where there is an RNLI lifeboat station and a disused lighthouse. It is a National Nature Reserve and also part of the Humber Flats, Marshes and Coast Special Protection Area and, like Flamborough Head, it is owned by the Yorkshire Wildlife Trust. Conditions are very different on either side of the spit, with the North Sea crashing onto a sandy beach to the east, and the much quieter, muddy Humber marshes to the west. The road linking the RNLI station to Kilnsea has been destroyed at the point where people are walking in the above photograph and the viability of this link, and of the Head itself, are uncertain.

**Above:** An image taken about half way along Spurn Head in 2015. The boulders, scattered like marbles, are the remains of Victorian coastal defences, placed in an attempt to stabilise the land against the power of the sea. The people on the horizon are walking on what remains of the track out to the lifeboat station.
**Opposite:** Looking west, up the Humber Estuary, from the Kilnsea end of Spurn Head. There is a Wildlife Trust Visitor Centre here.

## Conclusion

Although the Yorkshire weather could be challenging at times, causing me to chase scraps of blue sky, or wait for hours for the light I needed, the changeable weather also results in wonderful skies and a light which lends atmosphere to the lovely landscapes. Some excursions to collect images were treated as a bit of a holiday, some involved long walks, while at times I have driven from one end of the county to the other in a day, exploring lanes and byways, stopping suddenly (but safely) because I saw something of interest. Selecting the images to use from the large library of photographs that I have collected has been far from easy, and the fact that some lovely and well-known locations have been excluded results from the quality of my photography on the day, rather than the beauty of the location. In spite of this, I hope that *Yorkshire Landscapes* has succeeded in capturing the variety of scenery across the county, and that it gives as much joy to the reader as it has been to produce.

All of the images in this book were taken with Panasonic Lumix G-series cameras. I use a variety of zoom lenses, from the super-wide angle 7-14mm lens to the superb quality 100–400 mm telephoto lens produced jointly with Leica. These four-thirds format cameras are light and flexible, producing excellent images when hand-held: I hardly ever use a tripod.

## Acknowledgements

I am grateful to Cecil Snell of Scarborough Cricket Club for writing the foreword to this book, and to John Kedzierski for proof reading the text, using his linguistics training and attention to detail to correct mistakes and improve readability. I am also grateful to Wikipedia.com for providing a lot of background detail to add to that gleaned from the many Yorkshire web sites I visited. I also read Bradt guide books and visited tourist information offices for ideas for places to visit.

Finally, I am grateful to my publisher, Oxbow Books, and in particular to my editor, Clare Litt, for believing in my work and supporting the production and publication of *Yorkshire Landscapes*.

# Index of Place Names

**A selection of churches from around Yorkshire**

**Left:** St John the Evangelist, Cadeby; All Saints, Hovingham; All Saints, Settrington

**Middle:** York Minster

**Right:** St Nicholas, Bransdale; St Nicholas, High Bradfield; St Oswald's, Thornton-in-Craven

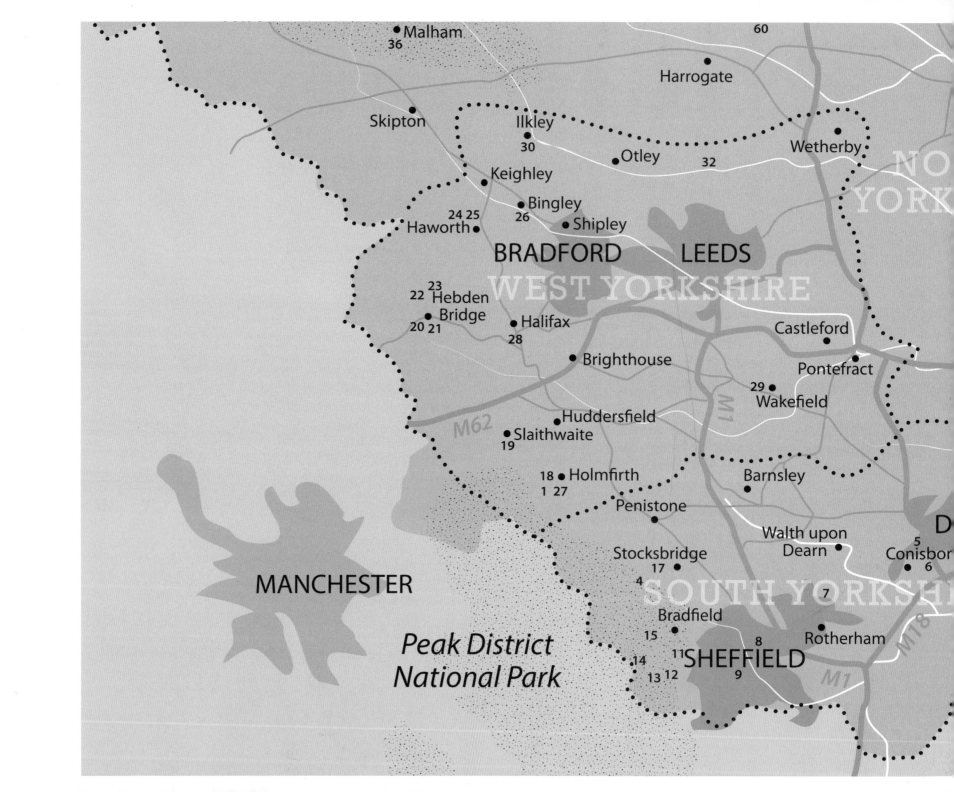